Corporatisms
Talk More, Say Less

John Necef and Hootan Rashidifard

*To our parents and siblings
for putting up with us from
the very beginning.*

Corporatisms
Talk More, Say Less

Table of Contents

Corporatisms
Talk More, Say Less

Table of Contents

Corporatisms
Talk More, Say Less

About the Authors:

We're two guys brought together by a passion to make other people smile.

As former NYC bankers and Silicon Valley "corporate ninjas," we know what it's like to circle back, add color, up-level, spin wheels, manage upwards, boil-the-ocean, peel-back-the-onion, and chop wood all while just taking a stab at a no-rush-but-want-it-on-my-desk-by-tomorrow-morning deliverable.

We hope our lexical observances lead to muffled laughter in the office and occasional reprieve from the daily grind.

Check out our latest happenings at www.lastlaugh.lol and @lastlaugh.corporatisms on Instagram.

-- John and Hootie

Introduction:

Here's what to expect. Each page will:

1. Identify a corporate "phrase"
2. Explain "how to use it"
3. Give an "example"

Different companies and industries have variations in corporate hierarchies. Here is a rough guide as to how we think about it in Corporatisms.

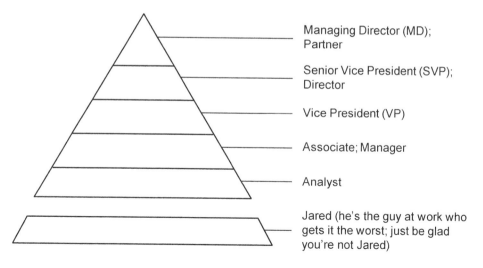

Managing Director (MD); Partner

Senior Vice President (SVP); Director

Vice President (VP)

Associate; Manager

Analyst

Jared (he's the guy at work who gets it the worst; just be glad you're not Jared)

Phrase:

"Illustrative"

How to Use It:

If someone is paying you millions of dollars for financial or legal advice, use "illustrative" to remind them that you're not confident enough in your analysis to take responsibility for any of the consequences.

Example:

Senior Vice President: Hey great work, but make sure you slap illustrative on every slide in the deck. We don't want anyone to make real decisions based on this.

Corporatisms
Talk More, Say Less

Phrase:

"ASAP"

How to Use It:

Always tell your junior team you need everything "ASAP." At this point, they know it's probably not true. But don't worry, the slight chance you're actually serious this time is enough to keep them dancing.

Example:

[Senior Vice President gliding by Jared's desk at 10 AM]

Jared, did you get a chance to watch the debate last night? Great. Also, hurry up on whatever I asked you to do yesterday, I said I needed it ASAP.

Phrase:

"Multi-tasking"

How to Use It:

Doing a million small things that add up to nothing.

Example:

Mentor: The key to success in this job is rigorous multi-tasking. You're not going to get sh*t done, but boy will you look busy and that's what we care about here.

Analyst: Sorry, what'd you say? I was checking my email.

Mentor: *[Sheds tear]* They learn so fast.

Phrase:

"Great experience"

How to Use It:

Force someone below you to accept any unwanted task by labeling it as a "great experience."

Example:

Hey Jared, great to have you on board this summer. We've got some mission critical work to get done. Can you go through the last four years of our client's public filings and highlight all of the Oxford commas? It'll be a great experience.

Phrase:

"How's it lookin'?"

How to Use It:

Fire drill! We've all been there, but you're an associate now, unwilling to lower yourself to do analyst-level work. While the analyst is cranking and you're refreshing Business Insider, be sure to irritate them by consistently asking "how's it lookin'?"

Example:

Associate: Now that you've had 15 minutes to build out the tax inversion merger model, how's it lookin'?

Analyst: *[Twitching and sweating]* Good.

Associate: OK. Let's hurry it up a bit. I'll check back in 10. *[Continues stacking paper clips]*

Phrase:

"Quick question," also disguised as "QQ"

How to Use It:

Be careful of this one folks. It's a trap. It's not going to be a quick question. Hell, it will probably be multiple questions. Use your knowledge of this corporatism on the defensive. If a colleague ever starts off by saying "quick question," immediately figure out some way to divert the conversation.

Example:

Larry: Hey Jim, I've got a quick question for you on the short and long-term effects of the Brexit vote on global commodity prices.

Jim: *[Punches own face]* Sorry Larry, something's wrong with my face. Gotta run.

Phrase:

"Let's take this offline"

How to Use It:

You're in a meeting with other people who start to get way too detailed. As you continue to get more confused, use "let's take this offline" to halt any opportunity for you to make a fool of yourself by attempting to participate.

Example:

Jared, I know the Vietnamese retention analysis is super important, but I think it's a little too detailed for this meeting. Let's take this offline.

Corporatisms
Talk More, Say Less

Phrase:

"Enjoy the long weekend"

How to Use It:

This is your boss telling you that he plans on absolutely obliterating you over the holiday weekend. Buckle-up kid. You better be ready to play the keyboard like Mozart on the bus ride to the Hamptons. At least you've been equipped with the finest 3G wifi and 27% battery life to get this done.

Example:

You: *[Chopping the keyboard like a lumberjack]*

Corporatisms
Talk More, Say Less

Phrase:

"Did you enjoy the long weekend?"

How to Use It:

Your boss is going to ask you this to make it seem like he cares about your life. He doesn't. If it seems like you had fun, he will take it as his personal responsibility to make you pay for it. Even if you didn't touch your computer for three days, it's crucial to make your weekend sound as unfulfilling as possible (but keep it believable, or he'll catch on).

Example:

[After three days of lawn games and day-drinking in Cape Cod]

Overall, my weekend wasn't bad. Had to plug in a couple times to format slides for Project Chatham and came into the office on Sunday to call the lawyers about diligence requests, but that only took up a few hours each day.

Corporatisms
Talk More, Say Less

Phrase:

"Short week"

How to Use It:

You got Monday off, might as well not do anything for the rest of the week. Slip "short week" into your conversations to push everything off until next week.

Example:

Manager: Hey Frank, can you take lead on the Ostrich Farm conversion opportunity?

Frank: I'll add it to my plate, but given the short week I won't be able to prioritize it. If urgent, maybe Jared can take a look?

Phrase:

"Let's handle this via email"

How to Use It:

Your colleague is super passionate about a new project. You don't care. When he tries to loop you in for feedback, suggest "handling it via email." You're never going to read the email. If you open it, it will be because you thought it was another email. But, you just successfully showed support by completely blowing him off. That's next level.

Example:

Wow, Jared! Leveraging zodiac signs to help forecast commodity pricing in Western Europe sounds super interesting, but I'm going to be jammed all week. Do you mind if we handle this via email?

Phrase:

"Disruptive"

How to Use It:

A last ditch effort to make something completely irrelevant and meaningless seem revolutionary.

Example:

Middle Manager: Our most recent business development efforts led us to a unique integration partner, AskJeeves. Their disruptive search capabilities will allow us to really amplify our growth.

Vice President: Great effort all around. I love the team's innovative thinking.

Phrase:

"Fwd to team"

How to Use It:

If you ever need to forward something, just have your subordinate do it. You've got better things to do.

Example:

MD to VP: Pls Fwd.

VP to Associate: Fwd to team.

Associate to Analyst: Fwd to team.

Analyst: *[After realizing everyone has seen the materials, forwards to self]*

Phrase:

"Broader macroeconomic trends"

How to Use It:

When someone asks you a question and you don't know the answer or weren't paying attention, "broader macroeconomic trends" will bail you out, guaranteed.

Example:

Q: Leslie, did you take the stapler from my desk?

A: It's possible, but I think it was primarily due to broader macroeconomic trends.

Phrase:

"The comps are noisy"

How to Use It:

You know your analysis is completely inaccurate, but have no clue how to fix it. Rather than looking like an idiot, deflect attention away from the quality of the underlying work by noting that "the comps are noisy."

Example:

Selling our new line of zip-away capris to the Jamaican market is filled with political and economic challenges, but the opportunity is tremendous. While the comps are noisy, we estimate that entering the market can quadruple lower-body apparel revenue by 2018.

Phrase:

"Just so everyone's on the same page"

How to Use It:

When in need of social validation during a meeting, say to the room, "just so everyone's on the same page," before recapping the key takeaways. They probably weren't listening to a single word, but you'll leave feeling great.

Example:

David Cameron: Just so everyone's on the same page, do we all understand the dire consequences of leaving the European Union?

Audience of Politicians: *[Mindless nodding]*

David Cameron: *[Smiles confidently]* Splendid.

Britain votes to exit the European Union

David Cameron: F***.

Phrase:

"Order of magnitude"

How to Use It:

People are talking numbers. Your boss puts you on the spot with some mental math. Panic takes over. Calm down, you've gotten this far without doing any mental calculations. Utilize those adept verbal skills and simply incorporate "order of magnitude" into your answer.

Example:

Well, I crunched all the numbers simultaneously in my head. Fully adjusted for tax benefits, forex risk and regulatory fees, relocating shell operations to Patagonia will increase earnings before taxes but after costs by at least an order of magnitude.

Phrase:

"Off the shelf"

How to Use It:

Your analyst is about to walk out of the door and you have a terrible staffing that will push him over the edge. Start off by saying you need a quick, "off the shelf" analysis to keep his spirit up. Once you have him modify it for a couple hours, completely change everything to get what you're really looking for.

Example:

Associate: Let's start with some off the shelf materials like that consumer internet go-to-market strategy deck.

Analyst: *[40 hours and two all-nighters later]*

Associate: Really nice work, Jared. This aluminum refinery cost-optimization model will really blow our client away.

Phrase:

"The midnight oil"

How to Use It:

Try not to use it. It's your youth.

Example:

VP: Don't burn the midnight oil, but I'm going to need you to read everything in this dataroom ASAP.

First-year Analyst: *[Looks up and it's his 35th birthday]*

Phrase:

"Do you have capacity?"

How to Use It:

This is a tricky one guys. You must say yes (make sure you sound stressed though) and simultaneously make it seem like you have less capacity than someone else, anyone else. Remember, you don't have to run faster than the bear to get away. You just have to run faster than the guy next to you.

Example:

Manager: Michael, do you have capacity to take on an accelerated IPO bakeoff?

Michael: I'm sure I can squeeze it into my workload. By the way, have you seen Jared? He mentioned he had time to help me print books since I'm also jamming on Project Purple, but I haven't seen him for hours.

Phrase:

"Kick it off"

How to Use It:

Check mate. You just got owned. You're in a meeting and no one knows what the hell is going on. By asking you to "kick it off," the burden of looking like a fool has been placed entirely upon you. You should always make the first move in these scenarios, but it's too late and there's no going back now. I hope you're quick on your feet.

Example:

[Jared walks into wrong meeting]

Other guy: Jared, glad you could make it. How about you kick it off?

Jared: *[Raises right hand over heart and begins Pledge of Allegiance]*

Phrase:

"That's neither here nor there"

How to Use It:

This might be the royal majesty of empty phrases. If it's neither here nor there, where is it? Let's just hope that no one tells you to find it because then you're really screwed.

Example:

Junior Consultant: Our competitive analysis shows SnapSnack's ephemeral grocery snacks business has been on a precipitous decline.

Client: Interesting point, but that's neither here nor there.

Junior Consultant: *[Befuddled]* But, but it's right here on this slide.

Phrase:

"Add color"

How to Use It:

You're on a conference call. Being silent for 20 minutes is a dead giveaway you're annihilating Candy Crush. It's about that time to show your value-add. Jump in at any moment and simply ask the person speaking, "can you add some more color here?"

Example:

You: Can you add some more color here?

[30 second pause]

You: *[Looks at desk phone, realizes call ended, shrugs and keeps Candy Crushin']*

Phrase:

"Tiger team"

How to Use It:

If you need someone to quickly do a bunch of undesirable work tangentially related to their job, tell them they're on a "tiger team." It'll make them feel like corporate Navy Seals, except in a fully air conditioned office, wearing business clothing, and accomplishing nothing extreme. Rawr.

Example:

After getting staffed on a tiger team to do a full audit of the division's internal expenses:

Jared: *[Wakes up with eyes already open, applies war paint, listens to Metallica en route to work, removes headphones, sits at desk, opens Excel, gently begins typing on keyboard]*

Phrase:

"High beta"

How to Use It:

If you want to make a last ditch attempt at sounding smart when you have no clue what will happen in a given scenario, say it's "high beta." It sounds mathematically precise and will intimidate most people from challenging you.

Example:

Client: How do you think the IPO market will shape up for the first half of 2017?

Senior Banker: Well you know, it's high beta. We've seen some winners. We've seen some losers. You really can't pin these things down. It's high beta...did I mention that?

Phrase:

"vFINAL"

How to Use It:

Ahhh, vFINAL, the deceptive final version tag which holds the potential to open the gates of freedom. However, labeling a document as "vFINAL" rarely works on the first try. It only moves you from the revision stage to the final revision stage.

Example:

Analyst:

[9:00 AM] Please find attached iChurn_vFINAL.

[1:30 PM] Please find attached iChurn_vFINAL_final.

[7:45 PM] Please find attached iChurn_vFINAL_final_v12.

[1:00 AM] Please find attached iChurn_vFINAL_final_v27_vFINAL.

[3:15 AM] Please find attached iChurn_vFINAL_final_v27_vFINAL_print.

Phrase:

"Tx"

How to Use It:

"Tx" has gotten a bad rap over the years, when in fact it might be the most desirable email response of all time. Many take it as a sign of a senior colleague's underappreciation or disinterest (both of which are probably true), but let's think it through:

You have just sent off what you think is a Da Vinci-level PowerPoint masterpiece. The email response can be one of the following options:

1. Changes so extreme that you might as well light your Mona Lisa on fire and start from scratch

2. No response, which either indicates (a) your "masterpiece" was so inadequate that your boss is embarrassed he hired you, or (b) you're anxiously waiting in purgatory only to receive response #1

3. "Tx"

I'll take number three all day.

Example:

Email from Managing Director:

    Subject: Re: vFINAL_final_v3

    Body: Tx

Analyst*: [Experiences a brief moment of happiness]*

Phrase:

"The weeds"

How to Use It:

Either you're in too deep, or you're not in deep enough. Don't take it personally though. No one has ever been able to effectively navigate "the weeds" because it's impossible.

Example:

[Jared's Q1 review]

Manager: Jared, you have the raw skills, but need to start grabbing projects by the horns and really get into the weeds.

[Jared's Q2 review]

Manager: Jared, you're spending too much time spinning your wheels on the details. You really need to uplevel and get out of the weeds.

Phrase:

"Let's keep this high level"

How to Use It:

Make this suggestion when you're utterly unprepared for a meeting and have a strong inclination that your counterparts are equally unprepared. That way, no one looks like an idiot even though everyone is an idiot.

Example:

You: Alright, I think we have a quorum, let's get started. Given the scope and complexity of Project Veneer, let's keep this meeting high level and take any specific or actionable discussions offline.

Quorum: *[Collectively suppressed smiles and muffled sighs of relief]*

Phrase:

"Quick favor"

How to Use It:

A "quick favor" is fish bait, and you're the fish. It's an innocent sounding ask used to trick a naive victim into becoming deeply involved in a project. Unless you're okay with getting reeled onto the boat. Don't bite.

Example:

Associate: Can I get a quick favor on an introductory meeting with a new client? It should be no more than switching some logos in our credentials deck.

[Four months later - the analyst is a junior member of the client's FP&A team]

Phrase:

"Just something to think about"

How to Use It:

When you want to sh*t all over someone or something, but don't want to sound like you're sh*tting all over someone or something.

Example:

Manager: Jared, things are going great. You're ramping up well. A few things to consider: your attention to detail is the worst I've ever seen, you single-handedly lost our client $100M, and you creep out the admins. Nothing negative, just something to think about.

Phrase:

"Ducks in a row"

How to Use It:

Have you ever seen ducks walking? They make a pretty sorry attempt at walking in rows. They're all over the place, especially the little ones. If your goal is to start slow with a mediocre outcome, comp against ducks. If you want to get something done well, stay away from this one.

Example:

Bottom Bucket Associate: Let's get our ducks in a row. We can start by brainstorming for a little while, jotting a few things down in no particular order, and having some meetings with no clear purpose or outcome.

Phrase:

"Throw in the towel"

How to Use It:

As an analyst, you don't control much, but you do control "the towel." When you're completely fed up with a project just throw it in. That'll really show 'em.

Example:

Analyst: *[Throws fifth towel of the day]*

Associate: *[Walks over to analyst bullpen, disregards pile of thrown towels, promptly pummels analyst with changes and updates]*

Phrase:

"Let's see how it looks"

How to Use It:

Your boss cares about you and your mental stability (just kidding). Rather than asking you to run a full blown analysis, he'll probably ask you to just do enough to "see how it looks." Yes, he knows you need to do the full blown analysis to "see how it looks."

Example:

Managing Director: Hey Jared, structuring this deal as a double-reverse, tax inversion could be interesting. Let's see how it looks, but don't kill yourself since we're going to move it to the appendix in v64 and drop it entirely in v73.

Phrase:

"Let's sync on Monday"

How to Use It:

What are you, some kind of overachieving MBA grad? Why do work now when it can be done later, next week, or never? Drop "let's sync on Monday" to clear your calendar for the rest of the week. Watch out though, acceptable delivery times vary by industry:

Corporate: after lunch on Wednesday

Consulting: post happy hour on Thursday

Banking: after 8:00pm on Sunday

Example:

Jared: Hey Gary, can we sync on Project Atlantis soon?

Gary: *[References empty calendar]* Sorry Jared, really jammed for the rest of the week. Let's sync on Monday?

Phrase:

"Get your arms around it"

How to Use It:

You've got a big, hairy project on your plate and have no idea what's going on. Start by telling your boss that you'll "get your arms around it."

Example:

You: Great, thanks for the full download. Let me take the next few days to get my arms around this and we can sync on Monday.

[Go back to desk, wrap arms around computer, check off to-do list, achieve efficiency god status]

Phrase:

"Throw it on my calendar"

How to Use It:

There are a few steps to this one, but if executed properly, your perceived productivity will triple:

Step 1: Always have the next seven days on your calendar completely double-booked.

Step 2: When a colleague asks to meet, respond with: I'm not sure, but find some time and "throw it on my calendar."

Step 3: GTFO before they take a look at your calendar.

Example:

Q: Hey George, can we discuss how to scale our supply chain distribution platform to Midwestern fulfilment partners?

A: Would love to Bill. I have to run to a mission-critical meeting right now, but find some time and throw it on my calendar.

Phrase:

"Do you have a minute?"

How to Use It:

For some unholy reason, whenever you get asked "do you have a minute?" you will always think "no" and say "yes." Be warned, some people's minutes are longer than others'.

Example:

[Friday afternoon; desk phone rings]

Director: Hey man, do you have a minute?

Associate: Sure. What's going on?

[45 minutes later]

Director: You think you can get that done by Monday?

Associate: Sure.

[Hangs up; calls analyst]

Associate: Hey man, do you have a minute?

Phrase:

"Boil the ocean"

How to Use It:

Oceans account for 321 million cubic miles of water on Earth. To boil that much water is literally impossible. So when you hear "don't boil the ocean, but…" you should feel comfort knowing you don't have to accomplish the impossible, only the nearly impossible.

Example:

Director: Jared, can you go through every large-scale biotech acquisition in the last ten years and pull management names and email addresses?

Jared: That will literally take me weeks.

Director: Jared, just make sure it's accurate and you get them all. That should be enough. Don't boil the ocean here.

Phrase:

"That's interesting"

How to Use It:

No it's not. "That's interesting" is a tactic to hush a subordinate who just said something utterly uninteresting. Pretty interesting, huh?

Example:

Associate: Jared and I ran the numbers and would not recommend an equity raise to our client at this time.

Vice President: That's interesting, but let's see how it looks if we completely re-run the analysis with one additional day of data.

Phrase:

The Royal "We"

How to Use It:

When you tell someone to do something, replace "you" with "we." You'll sound like a team player, but make sure someone else does all of the work.

Example:

Associate: Do you think we can get the kick-off materials done by tomorrow morning?

Analyst:

Associate: Ok great. Just let me know when we're done.

Phrase:

"Please handle"

How to Use It:

This one's for the senior professionals out there who want to have a little fun. Find a massive email chain, forward it to a junior analyst, and say nothing more than "please handle." Watch the analyst scramble to find something in the chain that needs to get done. It's hilarious.

Example:

[Global head of M&A to other global head of M&A]

The subject of the email chain was "Fwd: Re: Re: RE: FWD: Re: Project Atlantis," so I forwarded it to Jared…

…and all I said was "please handle!"

[pompous laughter]

Phrase:

"Underwater"

How to Use It:

To really drive home how overworked you are, use "underwater" to compare the feeling of a never ending workload to the feeling you get from being waterboarded.

Example:

Jared: Thanks for the new staffing, but I've been underwater for the last few weeks and not sure how much more I can take on.

Vice President: Well Jared, that's something you should really be working on. Some of the top tier guys don't even need to breathe anymore.

Phrase:

"Slam dunk," "grand slam," "home stretch," "Hail Mary," other misc. sports terminology

How to Use It:

Sure, you're working a corporate job to pay the bills until you get your big break, but the dream's not over. It's only a matter of time until you make it as a professional athlete. Be sure to use an abundance of sports terminology in the office to remind everyone where you're going, not where you are.

Example:

Team, we're playing in the big leagues now. Jeremy, Walter, Chet, I'm going to need you gentlemen to execute basic blocking and tackling while I quarterback. Get excited boys, we're going all the way with this internal memorandum.

Corporatisms
Talk More, Say Less

Phrase:

"Blacked out of pocket"

How to Use It:

Had a little too much fun this weekend? Use "blacked out of pocket" to explain any emails that may have slipped through the cracks.

Example:

Associate: Hey, why haven't you responded to my email from Saturday night?

Analyst: *[Checks phone and has no unread messages]* What email? I haven't gotten any emails from you.

Associate: Check again.

Analyst: *[Sees message marked as read from Saturday night]* Sorry, must have blacked out of pocket.

Talk More, Say Less

Phrase:

"Pencils down"

How to Use It:

"Pencils down" is a whimsical way of telling your team to stop working on something (throwback to 5th grade math class). Since you're being so funny and clever in your verbiage, be sure to tell your team to stop working on something only after they've completed it. You don't want them having too much fun.

Example:

[Monday morning]

Senior Vice President: Hey team, pencils down on the presentation for my coffee chat tomorrow with the CFO of Yellowstream. He canceled on Friday.

Associate & Analyst: *[Lock eyes in a moment of bittersweet solidarity, recognizing they now might be able to sleep that evening, while acknowledging the pain of a wasted weekend only due to a lack of consideration]*

Senior Vice President: Anyway, I've scheduled another meeting in it's place. Can you get me a deck by tomorrow morning?

Phrase:

"Massage"

How to Use It:

When you perform an analysis using the proper methodology, accurate historicals and reasonable assumptions, but it still doesn't come out to the made up number your boss has in his mind, you probably just forgot to give it a "massage."

Example:

Director: I agree with your assumptions and methodology, but not the output. Let's massage the numbers a bit to get ROI to 30%.

Associate: *[Questions self-purpose, suppresses existential crisis, slowly forces smile]* Ok thanks, that's great feedback.

Phrase:

"Think outside of the box"

How to Use It:

Clients want "innovative" solutions to their "unique" problems. In reality, they're all the same. If you want to provide real value, live inside a 2x2 matrix, rip your materials from previous work, and keep your solutions as mundane and efficient as possible. Just make sure you label it all as "thinking outside of the box" in the final presentation.

Example:

Vice President: Alright, the client wants us to think outside of the box on this one. Keep to our basic valuation techniques, but let's push boundaries and make the bullets in the presentation look like their logo.

Phrase:

"Entrepreneurial"

How to Use It:

If you're running an organization that has dehumanized the employee base for the benefit of shareholder value, keep up the good work. However, you still have to recruit new minions to do your bidding. So, just tell them how "entrepreneurial" the culture is. They'll eat it up like a delicious cupcake.

Example:

We have 250k employees and the role you're applying for hasn't evolved materially since the 1980's. Don't worry about that though, we maintain a highly entrepreneurial culture. We're basically a startup.

Phrase:

"Time to dig in"

How to Use It:

You can't dig in before the appropriate time. That would be way too proactive. Before seriously starting a task, procrastinate until the time *feels* right.

Pro tip: It often feels like a small ball of fiery cotton burning in the pit of your stomach.

Example:

[Looking up from his computer with bloodshot eyes after attempting to read the entire internet]

Associate: I just spent the last 6 hours reading Business Insider and can't remember a single headline *[deep breath]*. It's time to dig-in, we have a long night ahead.

Phrase:

"Rock Star"

How to Use It:

Call someone a "rock star" so they feel like they're doing a good job. They'll feel great right until they realize everyone is called a rock star, but that should be long enough to get what you want.

Example:

Vice President: Jared here is an absolute rock star. He's literally the best 4th-year junior analyst we've ever had.

Made in the USA
Middletown, DE
22 November 2019

79208685R00066